Still Her Daughter

A Daughter's Grief, A Mother's Grace

BECKY FENTON

authorHOUSE®

AuthorHouse™ UK
1663 Liberty Drive
Bloomington, IN 47403 USA
www.authorhouse.co.uk
Phone: UK TFN: 0800 0148641 (Toll Free inside the UK)
UK Local: (02) 0369 56322 (+44 20 3695 6322 from outside the UK)

Published by AuthorHouse 09/02/2025

ISBN: 979-8-8230-9473-3 (sc)
ISBN: 979-8-8230-9474-0 (e)

Library of Congress Control Number: 2025919507

Print information available on the last page.

I dedicate this book to my beautiful mum Yvonne Mander thank you for being my mum, I love I miss you so much. Rest in peace forever your daughter.

Sending love and strength to everyone.

Contents

Mum

Right from the start, you loved us with all your heart
You watched us grow and taught us to never be apart
We looked up to you with pride
Something we would never want to hide

As we grew, we wanted to be just like you
You gave us love an encouragement too
You are the kindest person we will ever know
The Angels have taken you, why is this so?

I know you are so proud of us all
That's why today we all have to stand so tall
Showing the world how fabulous you are
Even though you're gone, you're never too far

We love you so very much
Now rest in peace and look after us from above
And rest assured we will cherish your unconditional love

Without You

Without you, the sky never looks blue
Trying to live life and be happy
How to do that without you, I have no clue
The world keeps turning, which makes me snappy.

I look at your face only in pictures now
How can this be, you're no longer here with me
Life is not fair, trying to move on not knowing how
At last you are now pain free.

Before you went to heaven, we spoke for hours
I promised you I would live life the best I can
To remember you, I keep buying your favourite flowers
Just need to keep busy but nothing goes to plan.

I'm sat here now, not knowing what to do
Wishing you would call my phone,
I want to see your name
I know you will be up there looking
after me, that is true
Knowing what you are missing is such a shame.

A Mothers Love To my children

Being a mum is sometimes hard
Sometimes my heart even feels scarred
No matter what life throws at you
I will always be there for you, this is true

My love for you all will never die
I will do my best to never make you cry
You can talk to me about anything at all
I will always be there to catch you if you fall

I want you to know, I'm always here
I will always have a listening ear
So what ever you decide
Ensure you do it with pride

Never give up and follow your heart
No matter where you are, we are never apart
You will always have my heart forever
So you pick up that phone and call whenever

Love Mum

Goodbye

Today we had to say goodbye
Never did I think you would die
I would do anything to turn back time
Watching hours pass hearing the chimes

I wonder when I will see you again
Looking out the window, feeling nothing but pain
Wondering when I will let go of this strain
Looking at the sky saying goodbye.

Never will I forget you
When it's my time to see you, I will be in the queue
What I would give to give you a kiss
To fill you in with all that you've missed

Until the day we meet
I will always remember your heartbeat
You live on through me now
I will do you proud, this I vow.

Remember Me!

Remember me in everything you see
When you see butterflies this is me
I'm always there, showing you the way
You should never have a dull day.

When you think of me, smile at the sky
It's easier said than done but please don't cry
I am in a better place way up high
Looking down on you all just like a spy

When you feel like nothings going right
Please know I will be holding you tight
Just because you can't see me by sight
I will always be there even at night

I am your guardian angel from above
I will shower you with nothing but love
There is nothing better than a mothers love
So just remember I am always around you
So have no fear my dear
I am always here

Tears

Tears keep rolling down my face
Never did I think I would be in this dark place
Just wishing you were still here with me
But your not, how could that be.

Everyday the pain hits me in waves
One more day with you is something I crave
Nothing will stop these tears
I will most likely live like this for years

The amount of tears I've cried
I will always try to hide
Because I promised you I would be strong
But life is so hard now that your gone

I promise in time I will show happy tears
You not being here is my biggest fear
Still, I will be just like you, showing nothing but care
Even though life just does not seem fair

Life

Live life to the full, that's all I hear
I am trying so hard as my eye sheds a tear
Life seems different now not good or bad
Just seems my life is very sad
Without you mum I'm so lost
I wake up feeling so damn cross.

You gave me life which I am thankful for
But in my head I'm fighting a war
See living without you just doesn't make sense
The love and pride I have for you is immense

I guess I will carry on like you said I should
I promise you this, I will always do good
I will do you proud every single day mum
All I can say now is consider it done.

Yellow Butterfly

Beautiful yellow butterfly, I see you in the sky
So bright mid-flight, you catch my eye
I wonder if its you letting me know you are there
Taking a deep breath taking in the air

If it is you, please come back everyday
I will forever love you, let me just say
Fly free with no pain
Even in the cold and rain

When I have really sad times
I will listen out for your chimes
The spreading of your wings
Will forever make us think of happy things

Fly high beautiful butterfly

Why

Every morning and night I ask why
I just can't believe you had to die
The best woman I will ever know
Losing you hit an all time low

Why does God only take the good ones I ask
That must be one heck of a task
It doesn't make it easier, I'd rather you were here
But where ever you are, I'm sure you are near

My questions will never be answered I'm sure
But my memories will stay, no matter how raw
The angels are with you, holding you tight
I keep looking out for the feathers mid flight.

Summer Sun

Sitting in the summer sun alone,
Catching my breath
Knowing my worth, listening to the birds
Feeling the sun on my skin loving it to death
Resting my thoughts, not only my words

Thinking of my life choices back home
Knowing the struggle and sadness in me
My heart feels heavy like a stone
I wish I could stay here as I feel much more free

Watching the planes fly over ahead
While I sit writing this to clear my mind
Hoping when I'm home, all will
be fine and I'll go to bed
Waking the next day to start the grind.

My Person (Alex)

The night I met you, I knew I could love you
I didn't believe in love at first sight back then
But knowing many years later my love grew
I am so incredibly lucky, you are not like any other men

You love me so much I can really tell
I'm your everything and that is amazing
The way you make me feel, I know so well
That feeling you get when star gazing

I just want you to know I'm so grateful
You are my person and I love you so
I could never hurt you or be hateful
But I promise Alex, I adore you so much
I'm sure you know

Grief

When grief hits get some air
Take in a deep breath and let go
Why does it feel like I can't catch my breath
Drowning in sadness and disbelief

Feeling the sunshine on my face
Wishing you were here with me
Crying on my own, this is my life now
This is not fair I'm so angry

I sit and watch other people laughing away
Jealous of this let me just say
I miss you more every day
I never thought it would happen this way.

Dreams

When I go to bed, I know I will dream of you
Every night since you passed, that's all I do
Even though it hurts like hell
The love I feel, even though its brief, feels real

You look the same, so real to touch
When it's night time, I can't get enough
The sun rises and here we go again
Living life without you is so hard to bare

My darling mum, you live in my heart
I'll cherish our memories forever you see
I'm so incredibly lucky to have a mum like you
Even though I can't physically see you
You can see me

All About Mum

Blueberry muffin with a decaf tea
I would order this just for you
We would shop together, happy as could be
My god I would give anything to have you with me

Eating all your soft mints, you get mad
and say "don't eat them all"
I can still smell your perfume, like
you are still in the room
Rummaging through your handbag, all we
see is tissue, searching for your glasses
See little things like that, I took for granted
I will forever miss the things I thought was garbage

Cutting your toe nails seemed a chore
You were on edge, I knew this for sure
Lets go back to them times, not just in my head
When that day comes, it means I am dead.

Memory Box

Memories live forever in my head
Your belongings in a box, I can't bare to see
My phone rings, I think it's you
Then I remember there's nothing I can do
Except wish it was you

Your comb you used for your hair
The glasses you always had to wear
I always smell your lock of hair
The box of things that sit there

The love I have for you, is not in the box
All that love, lives on my heart
Something you taught me from the start
A mother's love, nothing compares
I'm forever grateful to be part of you.

Gods Plan

God has a plan so they say
Why does this have to be the way
My plans with you are now gone
It all just feels so wrong

Never in my mind did I think you would die
I really wish it was all a lie
But here I am writing this about you
Who the hell would have knew

Life goes on, the world keeps turning
Just nothing seems the same I'm just hurting
Rain or shine you are on my mind
Every day now seems such a waste of time

I'll get up everyday, live life in any way
Every now and then, I even pray
Hoping your well and watching over us
Sending us signals, advice that we trust.

Little Grey Jumper

My little grey jumper, still smells like you
You were the last to touch it, that is true.
I can't bring myself to wash it, I never will
So it stays beside my pillow while I lay still.

Hanging over your hospital bed, your hand on my head,
I wipe my tears so you don't get upset
Looking out the tiny window, waiting for sunset
Trying not to fall asleep, you have not gone yet.

I pray to god for some sort of miracle
But watching you fade away, knowing your not flexible
My world is crushing around me,
how do I live without you
You gained your angel wings so off you flew

You are loved so very much, this you already knew

X

Red Robin

Little Red Robin, I wonder if that's you
When days seem long and hard, I
just don't know what to do

You fly in the garden, it's like you know
I need a little pick me up as I feel so low

Some days I call your name, asking for a sign
Looking out my window, you are on the washing line

Feathers so fluffy, a bright red chest
The most beautiful bird, I feel truly blessed

Mum, if the robin is you, please come again soon
I'll listen out for your chirps, I long to hear the tune

Every time you catch my eye, I will smile so bright
All our special memories, I will hold onto so tight.

Stay safe little robin bird, fly high in the sky
I'm sure I will see you real soon as all I do is cry.

Emotions

Today I feel more anger than upset
Sitting here in the garden, not having regrets
Life seems hard and cruel, so angry you left
You fought so hard so it feels more like a theft.

Why did you have to go, the best person I knew
I feel like climbing the biggest hill
and screaming screw you
It doesn't feel real, this is what heart break feels like
Just like being stabbed with a sharp spike

Every ones grief journey is different I'm told
Even though the sunshine's warm, I feel cold
You see, Anger makes me feel bitter
Everything I do and see seems to be a trigger

So today I will stay angry and that's okay
Ride through this day, what a cliché
I will just do me, lets see what happens
I guess I will spend the rest of my life asking questions

Triggers

Some are good, some are bad
Many of these make me happy but also sad
This is now my normal, living like this
Why do I feel so lifeless

I can visit a place we have been together
The tears start rolling, I have to surrender
I listen to the radio, I hear your favourite song
Sitting beside me singing is where you belong

I long to hear your voice, giving me advice
Knowing that wont happen, my body turns to ice
To spend one more day with you, I would pay any price
Let me tell you now, you wouldn't have to ask twice

For now I will continue to live like this
Every day I will think of you, you are forever missed
I will embrace the triggers everyday
You always taught me to never run away

I am so blessed to have a mum like you

I'm Still A Daughter

I sit here today, I'm still your daughter
Even though you are now in heaven
You will always be my mum, my biggest supporter
Having the title daughter, is my biggest lesson

Mum, you showed me what love is
For this I will be forever grateful
Being your daughter is bliss
Living life without you is just so painful

You are on my mind daily, I will never forget you
My heart aches so much it physically hurts me
Your blood runs through my veins too
I'm always YOUR daughter, that's what I'll be.

My Protector

The hands that held me have gone
Just another thing for me to mourn
Who has me now..... I wonder
Feels like the fear I felt when younger

The uncertainty of who can I talk to now
Never did I think this would be the case..... WOW
When I need a cuddle, I crave your arms
No one except you could keep me calm

No longer having a mum crushes me so
Saying out loud "Your Gone" I just can't.... NO
Never will I feel the same, but il learn to grow
Now I don't have you, days do go so slow

I know I'm not the only one hurting
I guess I will forever be learning
So many people love you so much
I just want to be selfish and feel your touch.

The Day Everything Changed

31st of October was just a normal day
That's when our horror story started to play
I relive the weeks, it haunts me to this day
Everyone reassuring me, but what did the doctor say?
Never did I think that you would undergo such strain

I always knew you were brave, but
you went through hell
It seemed like we were living under a spell
I prayed so hard to a god I don't believe in
All that trauma and you didn't even win

Now you're an amputee, I didn't care
You were tired, I could see
I kept telling you everything was fine
Little did we know we were living a lie
I watched your body give up day by day
It was not supposed to end this way.

Noise

My grief noise, that's what I call it
Its hard to explain, I sound like a twit
My thoughts are fuzzy, like I'm on a fair ride
Everyone's voices seem to collide

The everyday noises seem more quite
Or maybe I'm just less inspired
Sometimes all I can here is my breathing
I'm guessing this is a small part of grieving

Now I know what real heart ache is
Just to get through each day, I feel helpless
My body is tired, I never felt like this before
But life is for living, that's what you would say, I'm sure.

Fading Away

Slowly you stopped talking
Your eyes stayed closed longer each day
Stupidly, even then, I refused to
believe you wouldn't stay
Hours turned into days, talking to you every day
Wiping you're mouth, knowing you are slipping away

Squeezing your hand, watching you lay
Hoping your now in heaven, and you have no pain
I hope you don't miss me, like I miss you
It gives me strength to think you see everything I do
My eyes feel heavy, full of tears
I'm sure this will carry on for years

I can sit here each day writing about you
It brings me so much joy, makes me smile
Even if its just for a little while
Never will I see you walk through the door
This crushes me right to the core.

6 Months On

The number 6 is just a number to some
But for me its 6 months since you passed, mum
6 whole months, that's half a year
Something I've been dreading to hear

It feels like yesterday since we spoke
I take a deep breath but it feels like I could choke
The first summer without you
How will I get through the next 6
months?... I HAVE NO CLUE

6 months, this doesn't feel long
Cant stop thinking how hard you hung on
I cant explain this feeling I have everyday
Given the chance, I would stay in my duvet

Knowing this feeling will never disappear
It fills me with dread and fear
Before you left you told me to be happy
Happy feels guilty, but il try to be less snappy.

Ashes

Picking up your ashes, a day I will never forget
The bag they were in felt heavy,
not what I was expecting
Taking you home, I sat on your bed
Holding you tight reflecting

Never before have I seen human ashes
To think that's all of you I just can't believe
Here we go again, tears rolling off my lashes
What happens now? I guess its time for me to leave

Weekly I buy you flowers
Wish I did this before
The guilt that I have now, I took you for granted
I sit and talk to your ashes, you are placed on the drawer
The next stage of grief for me has technically started

Until dad is ready, that's where you will stay
I can't lie, I love that your in your happy place
We will continue to live day by day
Never will we forget your beautiful face

Long Nights

While everyone sleeps, my thoughts
run around in my head
Every memory of you plays out like a slideshow
No longer do I feel at peace in my own bed
The night sky shines bright, the hours go slow

I could lay and count every star
I then start to wonder where you are
How can everyone else sleep but I'm wide awake
I often think, is it only my heart that breaks

You see the dark nights sky means
another day has gone by
Tomorrow night wont be any different
To think it will be different makes me sound ignorant
I will continue to count the stars
To be fair they are so elegant

The Best Version I Can Be

I think of you every day, but today has hit hard
Even though its hard to carry on, I'm still a mum myself
So up I get and struggle through, having
to believe in everything I do
I learnt from the best, I will be just like you

Even though your gone your spirit lives on
I am you, just a different version,
I will carry on traditions
With you leading me I will try to be
the best version of you and me
I will be forever sad, but for you I will have a plan

You are now in the spirit world
I still feel you here with me
I cry and smile at the same time
I'm just so thankful, and I will continue to shine

Love You Mum

Do You See Me

Do you see me now you are In heaven
What is it like. Where are you now? Is there any tension
Do you send me signs, I bet you do
Only the best mums would, that's definitely you

Are you watching with so much pride
I often sit and imagine you are sat by my side
Giving me the latest gossip, laughing away
Instead I'm here, all alone, waiting for the end of the day

If you can see me, I can't wait till I can see you
We will sit and catch up over a cuppa or two
Until that day my life will be ok
That's all you ever wanted, so that will be the way

Where are you now?

I ask myself all the time where are you now?
Where ever you are I hope it's not too far
To think you are not near me fills me with fear
If you're in heaven no longer shed a tear

Are you now pain free watching over us
Id like to think you send us positive energy and love
When I sit here day dreaming thinking of you
Knowing everything I do is to be like you

I can imagine how loved you are up there
Even though down here life does not seem fair
You honestly deserve peace now mum
So where ever you are, be happy but I'll stay numb.

My younger self

Today my heart continues to break
living in this world without you
Nothing I do or say can change that
I had to be strong on so many occasions too
Even to this day I feel so flat

No one else knows me like you do
I feel so lost and empty my life has completely changed
Going back to my younger self,
everything seemed fun with you
Even though at times you must have felt drained

If I could go back in time I would
even if its just for one day
I don't think I would change a thing, just remain
Telling you I loved you more is something I would say
To think all these years later, I'd be
writing this is just insane

Feelings

Losing a loved one feels like you have also died
Even though your still breathing,
A part of you died that day
Nothing will ever be the same as
before, you even want to hide
Holding a simple conversation feels like a heavy weigh

You never know how you will feel each day
How ever you feel is ok as its your own way
Nothing to prove to anyone else
My advise would be to concentrate on one's self

Everyone hurts differently, this I know for sure
I wish I had something to compare this pain too
Maybe then the pain would ease just a tiny bit
But for now ill carry on hurting like I've been hit

No dial tone

The clouds are moving fast above my head
Yet my world feels paused, nothing seems real
I still go to call you on the phone, no dial tone
Moments like this crush me, I don't seem to heal

Scrolling through the old messages
My heart aches but I remember those chats
Like it was yesterday, my best friend always
Even though you won't read them I
will continue to send them

Writing out the family calendar turns into a nightmare
Seeing all the dates that meant something to us
Never will I see your name in the same way
Just the anniversaries of all the sad days last year

At least I had your love all those years
Never will I forget shedding happy tears
Keeping your memory alive, this I will achieve
Never will you be forgotten, you're
light will shine for years.

To my readers

I love you all I want you to know
Even on my darkest days I'm thankful to you all
Always say I love you to the people that matter
One day sadly they wont be there even for a natter

When you read my poems they are from the heart
If they can help in any way I've done my part
You are all special in your own way
Continue to love and spread happiness each day

When the sun shines bright or even
on those dark rainy days
Be there for anyone in your special way
Take each day as it comes, live for those who cant
I'm so proud of each and everyone,
I'm shouting with a chant

THANK YOU
XXXXXXXXXX

About the Author

Becky Fenton is a first time author from Hampshire England, She is a happily married wife and a mum of three . The reason this book came to light was due to the great loss of her mum , Yvonne. Yvonne was cherished by all the family

This book has become a self healing diary for Becky and her family encapsulating all the raw emotions they are experiencing through their grief journey.

Beckys hopes are that someone somewhere who is or has experienced grief will take huge comfort in reading the poems.

Printed in Dunstable, United Kingdom

69035878R00029